Along Thimblelane Trails

By V. Gilbert Beers

Illustrated by Helen Endres
and Lois Axeman

MOODY PRESS • CHICAGO

What You Will Find in This Book

© 1981 by V. Gilbert Beers

Library of Congress Cataloging in Publication Data

Beers, Victor Gilbert, 1928-
   Along Thimblelane Trails
   (The Muffin Family Picture Bible)
   SUMMARY: Selected Bible stories accompanied by corresponding contemporary stories involving the imaginary Muffin family.
   1. Bible stories, English [1. Bible stories. 2. Christian life-fiction]. I. Endres, Helen; Axeman, Lois. II. Title.

ISBN: 0-8024-0298-4

Printed in the United States of America

To Parents and Teachers

Do you remember when you were a child? Did you have a favorite stuffed animal, perhaps a teddy bear or a rag doll? Did you ever talk to it and pretend that it was real? What child has not done that? And what child has not imagined himself or herself in a make-believe world with the stuffed animal friends?

This is a book in which Mini and Maxi Muffin enter that imaginary world of Mini's stuffed animal friends. They leave their shelf in her bedroom and go with Maxi and Mini along Thimblelane Trails. It all starts at the big tree by the Muffin Family picnic table. Where it ends...well, you must read the rest of the book to discover that. As you do, you will also discover how your child will learn Bible truth in action – side by side with the imaginary Muffin stories, which show that truth lived out in daily life. Children will relate in a fun way to Maxi and Mini, and to Todie, Widgit, Wumpkin, GiGi, Grabbie, and Snoggy. As they do, Bible stories and Bible truth will become a wonderful part of their lives. Other volumes in the Muffin Family Picture Bible series are *Through Golden Windows*, *Under the Tagalong Tree*, *With Sails to the Wind*, *Over Buttonwood Bridge*, *From Castles in the Clouds*, *With Maxi and Mini in Muffkinland*, and *Out of the Treasure Chest*.

GOING TO A NEW LAND

A New Home for Abraham

Genesis 11:27–12:9

"Moving?" Sarah asked her husband, Abraham. "Where? When?"

"To Canaan," Abraham answered. "My father, Terah, has ordered our tribe to move. We will start packing tomorrow morning."

In those days people lived together in tribes. When the head of the tribe said they would move, the people obeyed.

Nobody knows for sure why Abraham's tribe was moving. Perhaps they wanted to leave Ur because it was such a busy city. Or perhaps because their neighbors worshiped a moon god. Or they may have heard that Canaan had more food. Sometimes people wanted to start a new life in a new home far away.

Early the next morning Abraham helped to take down the tents and pack the family things. At that time he was called Abram. Sarah was called Sarai. She helped pack, as everyone else did.

"But so far away," Sarah must have wondered aloud. "And we will be alone."

"Not alone," Abraham told her. "The Lord will go with us. He will guide us there."

Before long every tent was packed. Every pot and robe was put in place. And every sheep, goat, donkey, and camel was brought together.

The people of Abraham's tribe formed a long line. Terah was at the front with his family and flocks. His sons, Abraham and Nahor, came next, with their families and flocks.

When everyone was in place, Terah started out. All the others followed. What a caravan that was!

Canaan was many miles away. It was almost straight west of Ur, Abraham's hometown. But Abraham's caravan could not travel straight to Canaan. A great desert lay between. They would not find water for the people or animals in that desert.

The caravan went instead along the river that passed by Ur. For many days they traveled north, following the river. At last they came to a city named Haran.

"We will camp here awhile," Terah ordered. The people were glad to set up their tents again. They were glad to let their flocks rest.

But many days passed. They were still camped at Haran. Terah did not give orders to move on to Canaan.

"Why?" Sarah asked Abraham.

"My father, Terah, is sick," Abraham told her. "He may not get well."

Before long, Terah died. Abraham and Nahor buried him there at Haran.

One day the Lord spoke to Abraham. "Go on to Canaan," the Lord told him. "I will bless you there and cause your family to become a great nation."

Abraham knew now that the Lord was with them. Sarah knew also, for Abraham told her.

Nahor stayed behind at Haran with his family. Abraham and his family went on to Canaan. The Lord went with them and helped them on their long trip.

When Abraham reached Canaan, the Lord spoke to him again. "I will give this land to your children and to all their family after them," the Lord said.

Abraham settled in Canaan with his family. Even though he was in a strange land, he knew that the Lord was with him. He knew that he would never be alone in Canaan.

WHAT DO YOU THINK?
What this story teaches: Abraham was never alone, for the Lord was with him, even in strange places.

1. Would you have been afraid to travel to a strange, faraway land as Abraham did? What if you knew that the Lord would be with you every moment?

2. Why did Abraham go on to Canaan? Why not settle in Haran as his brother did?

3. Is the Lord as close in faraway places as He is when we are at home?

Along Thimblelane Trails

"Maxi Muffin! Give me back my Buffy Bear!" Mini shouted.

Things like this sometimes happened when the Muffins ate dinner at their picnic table by the big tree in the back yard. As usual, matters went from bad to worse, and from worse to worst.

Nobody knows who started it. No mommi or poppi in the whole wide world is smart enough to figure out who starts what. It's always "he did" or "she did." As usual, Maxi did this because Mini did that. And Mini did that because Maxi did this first. So who can figure which "he did it first" or "she did it first" is really first?

Mini shouted when Maxi grabbed her Buffy Bear and ran toward the big tree with him. Maxi shouted back when Mini threw her glass of water at him. Then Maxi threw Buffy Bear high into the air by the tree.

But Buffy Bear did not fall into the soft grass. Instead, he popped into the big hole in the side of the tree.

"MAXI!" Mini shouted so loud that the leaves sighed. "Get my Buffy Bear out of that tree."

Poppi looked up when he heard that. He looked at the hole through which Maxi had thrown Buffy Bear. Then he looked at the big hole at the bottom of the tree. Buffy Bear lay just inside that bottom hole. He could reach Buffy Bear easily and bring him out. But first Poppi had an idea for some stories.

"I'll help Maxi get Buffy Bear for you," Poppi said to Mini. "But first, why don't you join him?"

"In that dark hole?" Mini asked. "Not me! I'm afraid of dark holes."

Poppi smiled. "You won't find Buffy Bear waiting in the dark hole," he said. "You'll find him on the other side of that hole, along Thimblelane Trails."

Maxi and Mini knew by the twinkle in Poppi's eyes that he had some good stories to tell. So they settled down on the soft grass to listen.

"I can't go with you on this trip," said Poppi. "You two will have to go alone…by pretending, of course. But as you do, remember this – the Lord goes with His people everywhere – even in strange places. And He goes with little people as well as big people."

In one pretend moment, Maxi and Mini were through the hole where Buffy Bear had fallen. They were floating down through the dark center of the tree.

"Maxi! I'm shrinking!" Mini cried out. "And it's dark in here! I'M SCARED!"

"Remember what Poppi said," Maxi reminded Mini.

Maxi and Mini landed softly at the bottom of the tree. They expected to see the picnic table through the hole at the bottom. Instead, they saw a strange path into a strange land.

"But I'm still scared," said Mini.

"Remember..." Maxi started to say.

"...what Poppi said," Mini added.

"Are you ready to come with me?" a voice said.

"MAXI! WHAT WAS THAT? WHO WAS THAT?" Mini asked.

"Let's ask," said Maxi. "And remember what Poppi said."

Maxi and Mini tiptoed outside. They looked this way. They looked that way. Then they saw who had spoken to them.

"Buffy Bear!" Mini shouted. "But you're as big as we are."

"No, you're as small as I am," said Buffy Bear. "Welcome to Thimblelane Trails. Would you like to go with me?"

"Yes!" said Mini. "And we WILL remember what Poppi said. Won't we, Maxi?"

So Maxi and Mini took Buffy Bear by the hand. Then the three of them went off along Thimblelane Trails.

LET'S TALK ABOUT THIS
What this story teaches: The Lord is with His people everywhere. He goes with the "little" people as well as the big, even into strange places.

1. What did Maxi and Mini mean by "Remember what Poppi said"? What did Poppi say?
2. Who went with Abraham into strange places? Who went with Maxi and Mini into strange places?
3. Have you ever been afraid in strange places? Next time, remember what Poppi said, even if you feel "little" or unimportant.

11

A Sad Day for Abraham

Genesis 12:10-20

"What will we eat?" Everyone in Canaan was asking that.

There had been no rain for a long time. Without rain, crops did not grow. Without crops, there was no food.

"We must move to another place," Abraham told Sarah. "We must go where there is food."

"To another place?" Sarah asked softly. "To another land?"

"To Egypt," said Abraham. "I'm sorry. We must go or we will starve."

As Abraham and Sarah came near Egypt, Abraham looked worried. Sarah asked him why.

"You are beautiful," Abraham told her. "Some Egyptian will want to marry you. He will kill me so he can have you."

"But what can we do?" Sarah asked.

"Pretend that you are my sister," Abraham told her. "Then no one will want to kill me."

Abraham was right. As soon as they arrived in Egypt, some men saw how beautiful Sarah was. They hurried to tell the king, who was called Pharaoh.

Before long Sarah was taken to Pharaoh. She lied, as Abraham told her to do. She told Pharaoh that she was Abraham's sister, not his wife. Pharaoh put her in a special place with his wives. Then he gave Abraham many gifts. He gave him sheep, oxen, donkeys, slaves, and camels.

Soon the people in Pharaoh's palace began to get sick. Within a few days they were all sick. Pharaoh knew now that something was wrong. He knew that this sickness had started when Sarah came.

Pharaoh called for Abraham to come to the palace. "You've lied to me!" Pharaoh told Abraham. "Why didn't you tell me she was your wife?"

Abraham did not know what to say. He knew how wrong it was for him to lie. He had not trusted the Lord to take care of him and Sarah in this strange land.

"Take your wife and get out of my country," Pharaoh told Abraham.

Sorry and ashamed, Abraham left Pharaoh's palace. Then he and Sarah left Egypt with all of the things that Pharaoh had given him. They went home to Canaan. It was a sad day in Abraham's life.

WHAT DO YOU THINK?

What this story teaches: When people fail to trust the Lord, they may lie to keep them from trouble. But lying may get them into more trouble!

1. Why do you think Abraham and Sarah lied to Pharaoh? What were they trying to do?

2. Did lying keep Abraham out of trouble? Or did it get him into more trouble? What happened to him and Sarah?

3. How do you think this story would have ended if Abraham had told the truth?

14

Todie

"Is that your Todie up there on the trail?" Maxi asked Mini.

"It is! It is!" Mini shouted. "But I thought that he was only a stuffed animal on my shelf, like Buffy Bear."

"Careful what you call me," Todie answered. "Otherwise I won't sell you this amazing Todemobile."

"What's the "T" for on the front?" Maxi whispered to Buffy Bear. "Todie?"

"He said it means Truthful," said Buffy Bear. "Some say it means Truthless."

"Doesn't he ever tell the truth?" asked Maxi.

"Sometimes," said Buffy Bear. "When he doesn't, his hat gets bigger. Watch the hat!"

"This Todemobile is brand new!" Todie said to his friends. "Just made for you!"

Todie's hat began to grow.

"It's the ONLY way down Thimblelane Trails," Todie went on.

Mini stood with her mouth wide open as she watched Todie's hat grow bigger and bigger.

"But why should I buy a Todemobile?" Maxi asked. "I'm not a toad."

"Neither am I!" said Todie. "Anyone can see that I'm a frog."

"I've always wanted to ask you about your name," said Mini. "Why ARE you called Todie if you're not a toad?"

"And I've always wanted to ask you about *your* name," Todie answered. "Why are YOU called Mini Muffin. You're not even one muffin, and certainly not many of them."

Nobody knew what to say about either name. So everyone said nothing.

"Now about that Todemobile. You must buy it," said Todie. "It gets eighty miles per gallon."

"Gallon of what?" asked Maxi.

"Who cares," said Todie, "as long as it gets eighty!"

"I'd rather walk!" said Maxi.

"But you can't walk along Thimblelane Trails," said Todie. "The snipes will snipe off your toes."

By this time Todie's hat looked positively silly. It was almost as big as he was. Now the three friends did not believe a word he said.

"It's the TRUTH!" said Todie. When he said that, his hat slipped down over his head. Mini started to giggle, but Todie ignored her.

"Only five hundred down and twenty per month," said Todie.

"Five hundred what?" asked Maxi.

"Who cares," said Todie, "as long as it's twenty per month. Look, do you want to fight off snipes all the way there?"

"There?" Mini asked. "Where? Where are we going?"

"Who cares," said Todie, "as long as you get there?"

Todie patted the Todemobile. For the first time Maxi and Mini and Buffy Bear noticed that it had dents and scratches on it. Obviously the wildest toad – or was it a frog – along Thimblelane Trails had driven it.

"Brand new!" said Todie. His hat grew some more.

"Well, uh, it was driven down the road a ways by a little old frog," he added. But when he said that, his hat grew so big that it dropped over him.

"Let's get out of here," said Buffy Bear. "That thing may swallow us next."

Todie was still talking as they hurried away. "Will the hat get smaller again so he can wear it?" Mini asked.

"When he tells enough truth to get it back on his head," said Buffy Bear.

"I'll never forget Todie and his truthlessness," said Maxi. "Especially the next time I start to tell a lie."

"And I'll never forget his hat the next time I start to tell a lie," said Buffy Bear.

"And I'll never forget the REAL reason we should tell the truth," said Mini.

LET'S TALK ABOUT THIS

What this story teaches: One lie follows another until we are in big trouble. It's better to tell the truth the FIRST time.

1. What happened to Todie when he told a lie? What happens inside you and me when we lie?

2. What did Mini mean by "the REAL reason we should tell the truth"? Who wants us to tell the truth?

3. How do your friends feel when you don't tell the truth? How do your parents and other family members feel when you don't? How does Jesus feel when you don't?

Givers and Takers
Genesis 13:1-13

Abraham was a giver. Lot was a taker. It had been that way since Lot was a young man.

When Lot's father, Abraham's brother Haran, died, Abraham took care of Lot. He treated him like a son. Wherever Abraham traveled, Lot went with him. When Abraham went from Ur to Haran, Lot was with him. When he moved to Canaan, Abraham took him along and cared for him. Lot even went with Abraham and Sarah to Egypt.

Through the years Abraham worked hard. He became rich. Then he helped Lot become rich, too. When Abraham built up flocks and herds of sheep, oxen, donkeys, and camels, he made sure that Lot had some.

Lot should have been very happy. He should have loved his uncle, who was a giver. He should have wanted his uncle to have the best.

But Lot was not thankful for Abraham's giving. Money had not made him happy. Flocks and herds had not made him happy.

Lot began to feel crowded. Abraham's flocks and herds were in the way. He wanted more of the good pasture for himself.

Before long the people who took care of Lot's animals began to quarrel with the people who took care of Abraham's animals. Then they began to fight.

"What will the neighbors think?" Abraham said sadly. The neighbors were the people of Canaan. They did not believe in Abraham's God. They worshiped idols instead.

"We're part of the same family," Abraham told Lot. "Family members should not fight like this! They should love each other and be happy together. Why don't you choose the part of the land you want? I will take what is left."

In Abraham's time that was the polite thing to say. If Lot had been polite he would have let his uncle Abraham have the best.

But Lot was not polite. He was a taker. He knew that Abraham was a giver. When he looked at the land he saw that one part had good pasture and plenty of water.

"I want that!" Lot said. He had chosen the best for himself.

"Then I will take what is left," Abraham said.

Lot, the taker, moved to his rich, well-watered land. Abraham, the giver, sadly watched him go.

WHAT DO YOU THINK?
What this story teaches: There are givers and takers. Takers are sad to watch. Givers bring us joy.

1. Which was Lot, a giver or taker? Which was Abraham?
2. How did you feel when you watched Lot, the taker, at work? How did you feel when you watched Abraham, the giver?

GiGi's Giving Service

"This is exciting, Buffy Bear," said Mini. "I thought you and Todie were just stuffed animals. Now you're real!"

"It's exciting for us, too!" said Buffy Bear. "We thought you were just a squishy person. Now you're real!"

"Speaking of stuffed things, look who's up ahead," said Maxi. "Isn't that your little stuffed gnome, Mini?"

"GRABBIE!" said Mini. "It's you! But what are you doing behind that silly booth?"

"I've set up business," said Grabbie. "It's Grabbie's Grabbing Service."

"But what are you grabbing?" asked Mini.

"Heh, heh, heh," Grabbie gurgled. "You haven't seen the booth next door yet."

Mini and Maxi had not seen it. So you can imagine how surprised they were to see Mini's stuffed calico goose with a charming little booth along Thimblelane Trails.

"GIGI!" Mini threw her arms around her stuffed goose. "But what is GiGi's Giving Service?"

"Just what it says." GiGi beamed. "I specialize in giving to the needy. We have so many needy gnomes around here. Or are they needy nomes? Or gneedy gnomes? Oh, dear, whatever they are, they have so many needs. The kind man next door sends them."

As soon as GiGi said that, Grabbie appeared, wearing a ragged top hat. "Pardon me, dear lady," Grabbie said. "The kind man next door sent me. I'm from the Poor Gnomes Without Homes Society. There are so

many poor gnomes who have no homes, so I'm collecting golden eggs to buy them some." Then Grabbie began to cry.

"Oh, dear, I have just one golden egg, which I laid this morning," said GiGi. "I wish I had a dozen to give you." Grabbie grabbed the golden egg that GiGi showed him and dashed into the back of his booth.

"That was Grabbie!" Mini whispered to Maxi. "Shame on him! He's being a taker, and poor GiGi is being a giver."

Just then Grabbie tapped at GiGi's door again. This time he had on a fireman's hat. "Pardon me, dear lady," Grabbie said. "The kind man next door sent me. I'm from the Fireman's Fund. It's for the poor firemen who got burned up in fires along Thimblelane Trails."

"How could they use the money if they are burned up?" Buffy Bear asked.

Grabbie thought for a moment. "Haven't you ever heard of widows and children? The poor little gnomes will starve in their mommies' arms unless I find a golden egg for them." Then Grabbie began to cry. Naturally dear GiGi the giver began to cry too.

"Wait! Don't go away!" said GiGi. "If I think sincerely enough about golden eggs, I'll lay one."

GiGi sat down in the corner on her nest. Before long a golden egg popped out with a very EGGS-citing "sproing!" Grabbie grabbed the egg and ran into the back of his booth.

"I just love to give to these needy causes," said GiGi. "Yesterday a gnome came from the Gnome on the Range Society. He wanted to fix all the poor broken-down kitchen stoves along Thimblelane Trails. The poor dear had a tattered cook's hat on."

While GiGi kept talking, Maxi and Mini and Buffy Bear slipped to the back of Grabbie's booth. They peeked in, and sure enough, there sat Grabbie, counting the golden eggs he had taken from GiGi the giver. And there on the wall were his hats.

Just then Grabbie looked up and saw Mini and her friends. He looked at the golden eggs. He did not know what to say, especially when he saw how angry Mini was.

"Grabbie's Grabbing Service is out of business!" Mini told Grabbie. "Grabbie's Giving Service is just starting. You will find needy gnomes or needy people who truly need this money."

Grabbie looked ashamed. "I...I WILL!" he answered. "Grabbie's Giving Service is in business and ready to go!"

LET'S TALK ABOUT THIS
What this story teaches: It's much more fun to watch a giver than a taker. It's also much more fun to be a giver than a taker.
1. Which one, GiGi or Grabbie, was more like Abraham? Which was more like Lot? Why?
2. Which kind of person would you rather have for a neighbor? Which would you rather be? Why?

JOSHUA- A MAN TO LEAD HIS PEOPLE

Tricked!

Joshua 9

"Joshua has captured Jericho!"

"What will we do?"

"We must fight him! Defeat him before he defeats us!"

The kings around Jericho were afraid. Joshua had captured Jericho. The walls had fallen down. But Joshua had not knocked the walls down. God had!

"Fight for your lives!" the kings said to one another.

The people of Gibeon had heard about Joshua, too. They were afraid of him, just as the other kings were.

"But if we try to fight him, we may lose," they said. "He will kill us if we do."

The people of Gibeon tried to think of some other way. At last someone had an idea.

"Let's trick him!"

"How?"

"Send ambassadors. Pretend they are from far away. Try to make a peace treaty."

It was a good idea. The people of Gibeon dressed some men in old worn-out clothing. They put on patched sandals. Then they put worn-out saddle-bags on their donkeys.

"And now for some dry, moldy bread," they said. "Also some old worn-out leather bottles. Then let's be on our way."

The men looked as if they had been on a long trip. Even a wise man like Joshua would think that.

One day these men from Gibeon appeared at the camp of the Israelites. Scouts saw them coming and brought them to Joshua.

"Where are you from?" Joshua asked.

"From a land far away," they answered. "We want to make a peace treaty with you."

Joshua knew he should never make a peace treaty with the cities nearby. God had told him to conquer them. But he thought it would be all right to make a treaty with people far away.

"How do we know that you are from far away?" Joshua's men asked. "How do we know you are not from a nearby city? If you are, we cannot make a treaty with you."

"Do you want us to be your slaves?" the men asked.

"No!" Joshua answered. "But you must tell us where you are from."

"We are from a land far away," they answered. "We have heard what the Lord has done for you in Egypt. We have heard what He has done for you in other nations. So our people have sent us here to make a treaty. Look at our moldy bread. It was freshly baked when we left. We left with new clothing. Now look at it."

When Joshua heard what they said, he believed them. The leaders of Israel believed them, too. So they agreed to make a treaty with these men.

But that was a bad mistake. Joshua had not thought to ask the Lord about this. Joshua's men had not thought to ask the Lord.

Joshua and the other leaders of Israel promised before the Lord not to hurt these people or their cities. Then three days later they learned the truth. These men were from Gibeon, a city nearby.

"We have been tricked!" Joshua and his men said.

Then Joshua and his men realized that they had not prayed about this. They had forgotten to ask God to show them what to do.

The people of Gibeon became servants. They cut wood and carried water. But Joshua and his people could never conquer their land as the Lord had told them to do. If only they had remembered to ask the Lord!

WHAT DO YOU THINK?

What this story teaches: When something is important, ask the Lord to help you.
1. Why did the men of Gibeon try to trick Joshua?
2. What would have happened if Joshua had asked the Lord about this? How might this story have been different?

Widgit and Wumpkin

"Thimblelane Trails is the greatest," Mini told Maxi and Buffy Bear. One by one she was meeting her favorite stuffed animal friends. But they were as big as she—or was she as small as they?

"Who will we meet next?" Mini wondered aloud. As soon as she said that, she saw her big Wumpkin sitting on a stump along Thimblelane Trails.

"Wumpkin, my Wumpkin!" Mini shouted. "But where is Widgit?" Widgit looked just like Wumpkin, except Wumpkin was many times bigger.

"Down there," said Wumpkin, pointing to a mossy maze not far from the foot of the stump.

"It's Widgit, all right," said Maxi. "But what is he doing?"

Maxi, Mini, and Buffy Bear watched poor little Widgit. First he went one way, only to come to a dead end. Then he went another way, only to come to another dead end.

"He can't see over the sides of that mossy maze," said Buffy Bear.

"So he can't find his way out," said Maxi.

"Poor Widgit, he needs help," Mini added.

"Yes, he does!" said Wumpkin.

"But Wumpkin, you can see the whole thing from your stump," said Mini. "Why don't you tell him which way to go?"

"Why doesn't he ask?" said Wumpkin.

"Is asking better than telling?" said Buffy Bear.

"If I tell before he asks, I have kept him from becoming an asker," said Wumpkin. "It's better for him to learn to be an asker than to find his way out of a mossy maze."

Buffy Bear propped himself against the stump to think about that. This is what he mumbled while the others listened.

"Widgit can't find his way. But Wumpkin can see clearly the way he should go. So why doesn't Wumpkin tell Widgit? On the other hand, why doesn't Widgit ask? Is it better to be told? Or is it better to learn to ask? Oh, dear! Widgit MUST learn to be an asker. So Wumpkin MUST wait and not be a teller."

Buffy Bear jumped up. "Wumpkin! You are right!" Buffy Bear said. "You must wait for Widgit to ask."

"But why can't Wumpkin tell Widgit to be an asker?" Mini asked.

"Then I'd still be a teller," said Wumpkin. "Even though I'm telling him to be an asker."

Everyone had to think about that one, even Wumpkin. So while they were thinking, the four friends watched Widgit work.

At last, Widgit looked up. He saw Wumpkin still sitting on the big stump, watching him.

"Wumpkin, can't you see which way I should go?" Widgit asked.

"Of course," said Wumpkin. "It's quite clear from here."

"Then why don't you tell me?" Widgit asked, almost with a touch of anger.

"Why don't you ask?" said Wumpkin. "Or are you asking?"

Naturally, everyone was happy when Widgit asked and Wumpkin told. Before long, Widgit was out. Then all the friends sat down to tell each other about askers. Or were they asking each other about tellers?

LET'S TALK ABOUT THIS

What this story teaches: Learn to be an asker. Someone important knows the way you should go.

1. Does Jesus know the way you should go more than you do? Why doesn't He tell you every morning exactly what you should do that day? Why don't you ask?

2. Do your parents know the way you should go more than you do? Why don't you ask them often which way is best?

3. God made parents to be tellers when children are too young to be askers. Then little by little they help their children learn to be askers. As they do, little by little the parents can stop being tellers.

4. When someone knows the way you should go, ASK! Joshua forgot to do that and got into trouble.

The Sun and Moon Stand Still

Joshua 10

"Kill the people of Gibeon!" a neighbor king said. He was angry when he learned that the people of Gibeon had made peace with Joshua.

What would happen to the other kings and their people? What would Joshua do to them?

"We must destroy Gibeon and its people," this neighbor king told some other kings. The other kings said they would help. Soon there were five kings with their armies, ready to fight Gibeon.

Now the people of Gibeon were afraid. How could they fight five kings and their armies?

"Help us!" they told Joshua. "Remember our peace treaty!"

How could Joshua forget? He had been tricked by the people of Gibeon. But he had agreed to help them if they were attacked. This time Joshua remembered to ask the Lord what he should do.

"I will help you," the Lord told Joshua.

All that night Joshua and his army traveled to Gibeon. The five kings and their armies were camped around the city. But they were asleep.

Just before sunrise, Joshua and his men attacked. The five kings and their armies were too surprised to fight back. They began to run away. Joshua and his men ran after them.

Suddenly the Lord sent a great storm. Hail fell from the sky. The five kings and their soldiers tried to run away from the hail. But they could not.

"I need more time to defeat these people," Joshua said. Then Joshua prayed for something that no man had ever asked before.

"Let the sun stand still," Joshua cried out to the Lord. "Let the moon stop in its place." Joshua and his men were in the Valley of Aijalon when he said that.

The sun and moon stopped until Joshua and his men had defeated the five kings. For almost one full day the sun and moon stood in their places. The prayer of one man had changed the world!

While the battle was fought, the five kings escaped to a cave nearby. Joshua found them and put a great stone over the mouth of the cave. When the battle was over, he returned and executed these kings.

Joshua and his men conquered that land. When they were done, they went home to Gilgal. But they would never be the same, for they had seen a miracle that no person had ever seen before.

"Thank you, Lord," Joshua must have prayed. "Thank You for giving me victory. And thank You for the great miracles that You sent."

WHAT DO YOU THINK?
What this story teaches: When we remember to ask Him, God will do great and wonderful things for us.
1. Why were the people of Gibeon afraid of the five neighbor kings? What did they ask Joshua to do?
2. What two miracles did the Lord do to help Joshua win the battle?
3. What does this tell you about prayer? What does it tell you about God's power?

Wumpkin Power

"Now what, little Widgit?" Mini asked.

Widgit was out of the mossy maze. He had learned to be an asker. That is, he had learned to ask his way out of the maze.

Widgit looked around. He looked at the big stump. He looked at the mossy maze.

"I like it here," said Widgit. "Now that I know my way through the mossy maze, I think I'd like to live here."

Widgit thumped on Wumpkin's stump. He poked here and poked there. At last he made a big decision.

"I will make my home in this big Wumpkin stump," he said. "All I must do is find the right place for a door."

Widgit went around the stump. He looked here. He looked there. At last he found the perfect place for a door. It was a Widgit-size hole at the bottom of the stump. But there was a Wumpkin-size rock in front of it.

"I'll move this rock and start to work on my door," said Widgit.

Widgit tried to move the rock. He pushed as much as a little Widgit could push. He shoved as much as a little Widgit could shove. But the rock would not move.

"Why don't you just pick up that rock and toss it into the woods?" Mini whispered to Wumpkin. "It would be easy for you. But look at poor little Widgit struggling."

"Have you forgotten?" said Wumpkin. "Doers keep people from becoming askers, just like tellers do. If I do this before Widgit asks, I'll be a doer, but he won't learn to be an asker."

"But I always thought that we should be doers," said Maxi. "That's what my poppi says."

"He's right," said Wumpkin. "But he wants you to be a doer of things you should do, not things some-one else should do."

Buffy Bear slid down beside the stump to think about that one. Wumpkin could be so confusing, or was he really making things clear? Buffy Bear had to think about that, too.

"But...but it would be SO easy for you to pick up that rock and toss it into the woods," Mini whispered to Wumpkin.

"It would also be SO easy for Widgit to ask," said Wumpkin.

It was hard to argue with that, so the four friends settled down to watch Widgit work on the rock.

Widgit grunted little Widgit grunts. He groaned little Widgit groans. But the rock would not move.

"This will do it," Widgit said happily. He put one end of a big stick under the rock. Then he climbed on the other end. But the rock would not move.

Widgit sat down by the big rock to think. "There must be a better way," he mumbled aloud.

"Wumpkin power!" Buffy Bear whispered, almost loud enough for Widgit to hear.

"Shhh," said Maxi. "Wait!"

"This will do it," Widgit said happily again. He put some string around the stem of a big bush and pulled. But the rock would not move.

Widgit sat down by the rock again. A tear came into his little Widgit eye. "I can't do it!" he said. "There must be a better way."

"WUMPKIN POWER!" Buffy Bear shouted, almost exploding. Everyone heard that!

But Widgit pretended not to hear it. He sat by the rock a while longer. Then he looked up at Wumpkin.

"You could pick up that rock and toss it in the woods, couldn't you?" Widgit asked Wumpkin.

"Yes, I could," said Wumpkin.

"Why don't you?" asked Widgit.

"I'm waiting for you to ask," said Wumpkin.

"I'M ASKING!" said Widgit. "Please..."

It took only a moment for Wumpkin to reach down, pick up the rock, and toss it into the woods. It took only another moment for Widgit to say, "Thanks," and get to work on his Widgit house in the Wumpkin stump.

LET'S TALK ABOUT THIS
What this story teaches: When the job is too big for us, let's ask someone who can do it.
1. When there is a mommi-size job or a poppi-size job that you can't do, whom should you ask to help you?
2. What if there is a job much too big for even a mommi or poppi? Whom should you ask?
3. We should be doers when the job is for us to do. But we should be askers when the job is too big. Mommi and Poppi are waiting to help. Jesus is waiting to help. Remember Joshua. He asked for big, big things, and the Lord did them.

WITH KINGS AND PRINCES

"We Want a King!"
1 Samuel 8-10

"Your sons must not rule our people," the leaders of Israel told Samuel.

"They take bribes!"

"They are not fair to people with problems!"

"They make people give them money!"

"They are not like you, Samuel. You have always let the Lord help you be a good leader."

"We do not want your sons as our rulers! WE WANT A KING!"

Of course, Samuel was not happy to hear that. He had always let the Lord help him rule Israel. But now he was too old. So he had told his sons to rule in his place.

Now the leaders of Israel were telling him some sad news. His sons were not good rulers. They were not letting the Lord rule through them.

Samuel was even more unhappy that the people were asking for a king. Why not another man of God to rule the land, as he had been? Why not keep on thinking of the Lord God as king, and His prophet or judge as His helper?

So Samuel talked with the Lord about this.

"The people don't want to keep on thinking of Me as their king," the Lord told Samuel. "If they want a man instead of Me as their king, then choose a man to be king. But warn them about the things a king will do."

Samuel called the leaders of Israel together. He told them what the Lord had said.

"You may have a man for your king," Samuel told them. "But he will take your sons to be slaves or servants. Some will work with his chariots. Others will fight in wars. Others will work in his fields or make his weapons for him."

"But we want a king!" the people kept on saying. Then Samuel told them more.

"A king will take your best fields and vineyards," he said. "He will take part of your crops. He will take your best olive orchards. He will take your best animals. Even you will have to work like slaves for your king."

"But we want a king!" the people kept on saying. Then Samuel told them more.

"You will cry when you see what a king will do to you," Samuel said. "You will be so unhappy that you will beg the Lord for help. But the Lord will make you keep your king and the problems he brings."

"We still want a king," the people said. "We want to be more like the nations around us."

"What shall I do?" Samuel asked the Lord.

"Let them have their king," the Lord answered. "I will send him to you."

Samuel did not know who this would be. He did not know that the new king was looking for his father's donkeys. He did not know that this man, whose name was Saul, would come to visit Samuel to ask about the donkeys.

Samuel was on his way to a feast when he saw Saul coming along the road. "That's the new king!" the Lord told Samuel.

Samuel waited while Saul caught up to him. "I'm looking for the prophet Samuel," Saul said.

"I am the prophet Samuel," he answered. "You're just in time to eat with me and stay overnight. Tomorrow you can go on home. But don't worry about your lost donkeys. They have been found."

Saul was certainly surprised that Samuel knew about the donkeys. He followed Samuel to the feast. He was even more surprised when Samuel gave him the best place at the table and the best food.

The next morning, as Saul was ready to leave, Samuel went with him to the edge of the city. There Samuel took some special olive oil and poured it on his head. That was called anointing. It was done for special people who were about to do special work.

"You will be the new king of Israel," Samuel told Saul. "The Lord told me to do this." Of course, Saul was surprised to hear that!

Later, Samuel called all the people together at Mizpah. He wanted Saul to stand before them. But Saul hid behind the baggage, for he was afraid to become the new king.

But some men found him there and brought him before all the people. "This is your new king," Samuel told the people. "The Lord has chosen him."

"Long live the king!" the people shouted.

The people had the king they wanted. But Samuel had warned that some day they would cry because of him. What they wanted most was a king. But a king was not the best for them.

WHAT DO YOU THINK?
What this story teaches: What we want most may not be what the Lord knows is best for us.
1. Why did the people want a king? Who had been the king before? How did the Lord rule Israel in Samuel's time?
2. What did Samuel say a king would do to his people? Why did the people want a king anyway?
3. What did you learn from this story?

43

Snoggy's Goodies

"Maxi! Look!" Mini shouted. "There's my Snoggy in that booth up there."

"That's some booth!" said Maxi.

"Yeah, look at all that junk food!" said Buffy Bear.

"Hey, watch what you call my goodies," Snoggy grumbled. "How would you like it if I called the stuff you eat bad names? Besides, take another look at all the delicious, nutritious, and just-plain-good-to-eat goodies."

"Yuk!" said Buffy Bear. "Candy, cookies, corn chillies, sundaes, and who knows what else is in that mess."

"But, Snoggy, who buys these goodies from you?" asked Mini.

"Who said I'm selling them?" said Snoggy.

"But then what do you do with them?" asked Maxi.

Snoggy picked up a big sundae with five flavors of ice cream, a double whammy of whipped cream, half a jar of Cherries Delight, and lots and lots of nuts and who knows what else on it. He downed it in two big gulps, as though it were a small glass of orange juice.

"Oh, Snoggy, I didn't know you were such a pig," said Mini.

"I'm not! I'm a Snoggy," he answered. "A Snoggy isn't piggy. He's just slightly hoggy."

Buffy Bear slid down beside Snoggy's goodie booth to think about that. "What's the difference?" he mumbled.

"To be piggy is to be muddy dirty," said Snoggy. "You know, the kind that takes an afternoon nap in a barnyard mud puddle. Snoggy doesn't do things like that."

"Then what does Snoggy do?" asked Maxi.

"Snogs," said Snoggy. "Then he snogs some more. And when he's through with that, he starts all over again."

"And that's being hoggy instead of piggy?" asked Buffy Bear.

"You might say so," Snoggy answered. "Or you might say it's being snoggy."

"But, Snoggy, all that junk food isn't good for you," Mini argued. "You might get cancer or flat feet or CLOR-EP-STOOL."

"Cholesterol," Buffy Bear corrected.

"That's what I said," Mini answered. "Anyway, he might get fat or something."

"GET fat?" Maxi and Buffy Bear chimed in together.

"How can you get what you already are?"

Snoggy paid no attention to them. Instead, he picked up a giant-size candy bar and a bag of corn chillies and snogged them down.

"But, Snoggy! If you eat all this stuff all the time it just can't be good for you," said Mini. "So why do you do it?"

"Because Snoggy LIKES Snoggy's goodies," he answered. "If I want them, I should eat them."

"I suppose you would eat a rhino if you wanted one," Buffy Bear argued.

"Hm. Haven't tried that," said Snoggy. "Might be good at that. If I want it, I'll eat it." With that, Snoggy picked up a giant jar of jelly beans and snogged them down like a vacuum cleaner.

"We've got to do something!" Mini whispered to Maxi and Buffy Bear. "What can we do to show him that it's best to WANT what's best for him?"

"I have an idea," said Buffy Bear. "I just happen to have THIS in my pocket."

"Pepper!" said Maxi. "But what will you do with that?"

"Watch!" said Buffy Bear. Then he held his jar of pepper up for Snoggy to see.

"Ever had any of this?" Buffy Bear asked Snoggy. "It is the most exciting, taste-tingling, red hot thing that's going." Buffy Bear kept on saying things like that about the pepper. Before long Snoggy began to drool. "But it's NOT good for you!" Buffy Bear added.

"Who cares! Snoggy wants some anyway," Snoggy said. Then he grabbed the jar from Buffy Bear and snogged the whole thing down in one gulp.

Tears began to stream down Snoggy's cheeks. Mini thought for sure that she saw red smoke coming out of Snoggy's ears. With a "YA-HOO," Snoggy jumped into a nearby pond and drank almost the whole thing.

"NOT good for Snoggy," he said to Buffy Bear.

"I told you so!" said Buffy Bear. "But you WANTED it anyway, didn't you? And you said everything you want is good for you."

Snoggy thought about that. Then he thought some more about it. At last Snoggy tacked a sign over his booth. It said "SNOGGY'S GOODIES FOR SALE."

"From now on, Snoggy will want things that are best for Snoggy," he said.

LET'S TALK ABOUT THIS

What this story teaches: It's best to want what's best for us.

1. Why did Snoggy eat so many of his goodies at first? What did he say?

2. What caused Snoggy to change his mind?

3. Who knows best what is best for you? Does Jesus? Do your parents?

4. Think of three things that were worst for you last week. What will you do about them next week? Now think of three things that were best for you last week. What will you do about them next week?

5. The people of Israel wanted a king, even though Samuel told them that a king was not best for them. Who would have been best for them?

"I Can't Wait!"
1 Samuel 13:1–14

"Have you heard the news?"

"What news?"

"Jonathan attacked the Philistine fort at Geba! He destroyed it!"

"But what will the Philistines do now?"

What would the Philistines do now? The people of Israel buzzed with excitement. Prince Jonathan, King Saul's son, had stirred up trouble. Surely the Philistines would fight back.

"If they do, they will destroy us," some said. "They have more soldiers than we do. They have better weapons than we do. How can we hope to win?"

The people of Israel were sure of one thing. It was time to get their army together. They soon had their best soldiers camped at Gilgal.

The Philistines quickly got their army together, too. Before long they were camped a few miles north at Michmash.

But the Philistines had a much larger army than the people of Israel. They had thousands of chariots and horsemen. They had many thousands of soldiers.

When the soldiers of Israel saw the Philistines, they were afraid. They were so afraid that they began to run away.

Some hid in caves. Others hid behind bushes. Still others hid among rocks and tombs. A few fled all the way across the Jordan River.

By this time King Saul was afraid. "Where is Samuel?" he asked. Samuel had told Saul he would come in seven days and make an offering to the Lord. This was the seventh day.

"I CAN'T WAIT!" Saul said. "I must make the offering to the Lord!"

Saul's men began to whisper. They knew this was wrong. Only Samuel should make offerings to the Lord. He was God's prophet in Israel.

"Saul knows this is wrong!"

"Samuel told him to wait!"

"I can't wait!" Saul said again. Then he began to make the offering without Samuel.

As Saul was finishing the offering, who should come along but Samuel. Saul hurried out to meet him and tried to explain.

"What have you done?" Samuel asked.

Saul began to make excuses.

"I could not wait!" Saul answered. "My men were running away."

"But the Lord didn't run away," Samuel must have answered. Then Samuel gave Saul the sad news about a king who could not wait.

"You have not obeyed the Lord," Samuel said. "How can the Lord have a king over Israel who can't obey Him?"

Saul hung his head. Samuel told him that another man would be king some day.

"Your children and grandchildren will not be kings forever, as God had wanted them to be," Samuel said.

Saul knew he was wrong. He should have waited. He was sorry now for what he had done. But it was too late.

WHAT DO YOU THINK?

What this story teaches: When God wants us to wait, it is a good idea to wait, even though we want to rush ahead.

1. Why was Saul wrong when he made the offering?
2. Why do you think it was hard for Saul to wait? What was Saul's punishment?

Tame That Todemobile!

"What's that noise?" Buffy Bear asked. He looked up Thimblelane Trails. He looked down Thimblelane Trails. Then he saw what was making the noise. Maxi and Mini saw what was making the noise, too.

"Oh, no!" said Buffy Bear. "Look what's coming!"

"Todie!" said Mini.

"And his Todemobile!" said Maxi. "Look at the way he drives that thing. No wonder it's beat up."

Todie wasn't exactly the most careful driver Maxi and Mini had seen. In fact, he was positively wild.

"*Vroom! Vroom!*" the Todemobile went as Todie revved up its todepower engine. Maxi wondered how he ever got eighty miles per gallon doing that. But then, Todie had never told him the answer to "a gallon of what?"

"Thought you would like to see this thing in action," said Todie as he drove up. "Listen to the purr of that engine."

"Sounds like it's croaking to me," Buffy Bear told him.

"Croaking is purring to us frogs," said Todie. "I just thought you wouldn't understand if I told you to listen to the croaking of that engine. Now watch what it will do. Then you will want to buy it."

"WAIT!" said Maxi. "We want to talk with you."

"Can't wait," said Todie. "I've got to show you."

Todie vroomed the engine at top speed and roared down the trail. Then he roared back.

"Now I'll show you how the horn works!" Todie boasted. "Horns always make people buy!"

"WAIT!" said Maxi. "We want to talk with you."

But Todie wouldn't wait. Instead he laid on the horn. It croaked and grunked like a gigantic frog pond. Todie smiled a big smile when he heard all this croaking and grunking.

"Sweet music, isn't it?" he asked.

"Yuk!" Buffy Bear whispered to Maxi and Mini.

"Now for a demonstration that will absolutely make you want to buy it," said Todie. "This beautiful machine will stop on a dime. Watch!"

"WAIT!" said Maxi. "We want to talk with you."

"Can't wait," said Todie. "Got to show you how these brakes work!"

Without waiting to hear what Maxi had to say, Todie vroomed the engine again and roared down Thimblelane Trails.

"WAIT!" Maxi called. "Stop!"

But Todie only vroomed the engine more. Then suddenly he slammed on the brakes.

Dust flew.

Wheels screeched.

Buffy Bear covered his ears.

Mini covered her eyes.

The Todemobile swerved, and before anyone could say anything, it headed for a pond by the trail. Maxi and Mini and Buffy Bear ran to see what had

happened. There was the Todemobile, half stuck in the pond. And there was Todie, dangling his feet in the water.

"Why didn't you wait?" Maxi asked. "We could have saved you some trouble."

"Well, here I am," said Todie. "What did you have to say?"

"Why try to sell us a Todemobile when we have no money to pay for it?" Maxi asked. "Why rush here and rush there showing us that thing when we can't buy it?"

Todie splashed his foot in the pond. He hadn't thought about those things. All he had thought about was selling the Todemobile.

"Well, I certainly learned something," said Buffy Bear. "There's a time to rush and a time to wait. We shouldn't be rushing when we should be waiting."

"I learned something too," said Mini. "Todie needs help getting that thing out of the pond. So let's help!" And that's what they did.

LET'S TALK ABOUT THIS

What this story teaches: Don't rush ahead when you should be waiting.

1. In the Bible story, how did Saul rush ahead when he should have been waiting? In this story, how did Todie rush ahead when he should have been waiting?
2. Can you think of a time when you rushed ahead when you should have waited? Think about that next time you want to rush ahead.

"The Lord Will Help Us!"
1 Samuel 14:1–23

"Come with me," Prince Jonathan told the young man who carried his armor.

"Where are we going?"

"Sh! We're leaving our army camp here at Gibeah! We have a secret work to do!"

The young man followed Prince Jonathan without another question.

Jonathan's father, King Saul of Israel, had been camped there for several days. He had gathered the soldiers of Israel with him. The Philistines had gathered their soldiers and set up camp to the north, at Michmash.

But Saul's soldiers were afraid. Many of them ran away and hid. They saw the thousands of Philistines and were afraid of being killed.

The soldiers of Israel were afraid to attack the Philistines. For some reason, the Philistines did not attack the Israelites. The two armies stayed in their camps.

Prince Jonathan decided to do something about this. He took with him the young man who carried his armor. He slipped quietly from the camp and headed north, toward the Philistines. No one, not even King Saul, knew that he was going.

Jonathan and his helper came to a deep gorge. "Look!" said Jonathan. "The Philistines are camped on the other side."

"But where are we going?" asked the young man. "What are we going to do?"

"We are going to climb up there," Jonathan answered. "Perhaps THE LORD WILL HELP US. He doesn't care how many Philistines there are."

That was a very brave thing for Prince Jonathan to say. Not many young men will attack an army alone. No wonder he said, "The Lord will help us."

"I will go with you," the young man said.

"Good!" said Jonathan. "Now, when they see us we will let them speak first. If they tell us to stay here, we'll wait to fight them here. If they tell us to come up, we will know the Lord will help us fight them there."

Before long the Philistines saw Jonathan and the young man climbing up the gorge toward them. "Come up here and we will fight you," they said.

"Let's go!" said Jonathan. "The Lord will help us fight them and win!"

As soon as Jonathan and the young man reached the top, they began to fight. They swung their swords here and there. The Philistines were suddenly afraid. They didn't need to be afraid of two men. But the thousands of Philistines were so afraid that they began to fight each other.

Then Jonathan and the young man knew that the Lord was helping them.

Suddenly an earthquake rumbled. The Philistines were even more afraid. The Lord was helping Jonathan and the young man again.

Saul's scouts saw the Philistines running away. They saw many fighting each other. So they quickly told Saul.

"Find out who is missing!" Saul ordered. Soon they knew that it was Jonathan and his helper.

"Bring the Ark of God and the priest," Saul ordered again. Then he quickly asked the priest what the Lord said.

Things began to happen fast. Saul's soldiers joined in the battle fighting the Philistines. Some of Saul's men who had been forced to join the Philistine army began to fight them, too. Then the people who had run away from Saul's army came back. They began to fight the Philistines.

The battle was fierce, but the Lord helped the people of Israel. Two men had brought a great victory to Israel – but only because the Lord had helped them.

WHAT DO YOU THINK?

What this story teaches: The Lord can help us do much more than we can do ourselves.

1. Why did Jonathan and his helper attack the Philistines alone? Who did they expect would help them?

2. What kind of help did the Lord give? How do you think this story would have ended without the Lord's help?

Wumpkin's Can Company

"There's my Wumpkin again," said Mini.

"What is he doing with all those cans?" asked Maxi.

"Let's ask," said Buffy Bear.

"Wumpkin, Wumpkin," said Mini. "Why all the cans?"

Wumpkin looked up and smiled a Wumpkin smile at Mini and her friends. "They are part of my can company," he said.

"But what do you can?" asked Maxi.

"CAN'TS," said Wumpkin. As soon as he said that, he reached up near his mouth, took the word CAN'TS, and popped it into a can. Then he put a lid on the can and sealed it.

"But you CAN'T do that," said Mini.

As soon as Mini said that, Wumpkin reached up near her mouth and took her CAN'T. He popped it into a can and sealed it.

Buffy Bear scratched his head. He propped himself against a tree to think about this.

"How CAN someone can CAN'TS?" he mumbled.

"That's a little one," said Wumpkin, reaching for Buffy Bear's CAN'T mumble. "I could almost squeeze two of those in a can." But he canned it in one of his cans anyway.

"Do you only can CAN'TS?" asked Mini.

"Yup!" said Wumpkin, grabbing Mini's CAN'T before it blew away and canning it in a CAN'T can.

"But why don't you can CANS?" asked Maxi.

"No need to," said Wumpkin. "They're already CANS. Why can CANS when they're already CANS?"

"But why can CAN'TS?" asked Buffy Bear.

"Why can CAN'TS?" Wumpkin repeated, stuffing the last two CAN'TS into a CAN'T can. "I thought you knew. Canning CAN'TS turns them into CANS."

Buffy Bear was still propped against the tree, trying to think about all this. It was really quite a lot of cans and CAN'TS and CANS for a stuffy head.

"Which CANS does it turn them into?" Maxi asked. "Tin cans or CAN CANS?"

"It turns I CAN'TS into I CANS," said Wumpkin.

Maxi thought for a moment. "That reminds me of the Bible story Poppi read the other day," he said. "Everyone in King Saul's army said, 'I CAN'T fight the Philistines.' But Prince Jonathan said, 'I CAN and GOD CAN.' So he and God fought them and won."

"See?" said Wumpkin. "He canned all the other I CAN'TS. When he opened them he had an I CAN."

"And a GOD CAN!" added Mini.

"So you see, Wumpkin's Can Company really works!" said Wumpkin. "I told you so."

Buffy Bear was still scratching his head. He was still trying to figure out all of this. Then Buffy Bear started to say, "I CAN'T understand this." But Wumpkin grabbed his I CAN'T and popped it into a can. Then he opened a CAN can and put an I CAN up near Buffy Bear where the I CAN'T had been. Imagine how surprised Buffy Bear was to hear himself say, "I CAN understand this."

Maxi and Mini laughed. Buffy Bear laughed too. Then the three friends waved good-bye to Wumpkin and his can company (or was it a CAN company?) and went on along Thimblelane Trails. Now each was talking about what I CAN do and what GOD CAN do.

Nobody wanted to talk about what I CAN'T do. They knew if they did, Wumpkin would can their CAN'TS and turn them into CANS.

LET'S TALK ABOUT THIS
What this story teaches: Don't say, "I CAN'T," when God is helping you. GOD CAN and YOU CAN when you let Him work through you.
1. In the Bible story, did Jonathan think *I CAN* or *I CAN'T?* Did he think *GOD CAN* or *GOD CAN'T?*
What did the other soldiers in Saul's army think?
2. Have you ever thought *I CAN'T?* Try thinking *GOD CAN* next time. I CAN is good for Mini- and Maxi-size jobs. But when the job is too big, GOD CAN. Ask Him!

A TIME TO FOLLOW

Let's Go Fishing!

Luke 5:1–8

"Let's go fishing," Peter said to his partners, Andrew, James, and John. The four fishermen went fishing almost every night, for that was their job.

As the sun was setting, two men climbed into each of their two fishing boats and headed for deep water. At night the fish came up to the top. The fishermen could catch them with their nets.

At the right place the four threw out the big nets. Then they brought the nets in, watching for fish. But there was not one fish in them.

The fishermen threw out the nets again. But again there was not a fish. Again and again they threw out their nets and pulled them back to the boats. But each time they caught nothing.

This went on all night until the first light of morning appeared. The fishermen were tired and discouraged.

"Let's go home!" Peter grumbled at last. "There's not a fish in the sea!"

The others nodded. They knew there were many fish in the Sea of Galilee. But they were tired and ready to quit.

When the nets were pulled into the boats, the four headed for shore. It would be no fun to wash the nets now that they had caught no fish. But it was a job that had to be done.

The boats touched shore, and the men threw out their nets. Already the village of Capernaum was awake and dozens of people were going about their work.

As the four fishermen washed their nets they almost forgot about the others. But suddenly Peter looked up. There was Jesus, watching the four wash the nets. Behind Jesus, crowds of people were gathering to see what He would do or hear what He would say.

The people kept crowding closer and closer and almost pushed Jesus into the sea. "Let's get into your boat," Jesus said to Peter.

Peter was tired of his boat, but he would do anything for Jesus. Within a few minutes he and his partners had moved their fishing boat a few feet from shore. Now the people could not push or shove Jesus. And Jesus could quietly teach them while He sat in the boat.

When Jesus finished teaching the people, He spoke to the four fishermen. "Let's go fishing!" He said. "Move the boat to deeper water!"

Peter must have groaned when he heard that. Who wanted to fish now? But if Jesus said to fish, they would fish.

The fishermen must have looked very discouraged as they sailed slowly to deeper water. But they had not gone far when Jesus told them to stop.

"Throw out your nets!" Jesus said.

"But we have thrown out our nets all night!" Peter argued. "We didn't catch one fish!"

Jesus said nothing. He quietly watched as the fishermen slowly threw out their nets.

Suddenly the water seemed to come alive. Dozens of silver streaks flashed in the morning sun, just below the waves.

"Look at those fish!" Peter cried out.

"Pull the nets! Hurry!" shouted another.

The fishermen pulled with all their might. As they dragged the nets filled with fish into the boat, they were amazed. The nets were so full they were tearing.

There were so many fish that the boat almost sank. It was time to go home.

As the boat sailed slowly back to Capernaum, Peter and his friends sat down to rest. But Peter stared at Jesus, sitting at the other end of the boat.

"How did He do it?" he kept asking himself. But by the time they reached shore, Peter was sure that he knew the answer. Jesus was more than a man. He must surely be God's Son.

When the boat reached shore, Peter jumped out. As Jesus came from the boat, Peter knelt before Him.

"Leave me, Lord," he begged. "I am a sinful man."

Jesus smiled. He must have thought of all the wonderful miracles these fishermen would see Him do. They had many exciting things ahead of them!

WHAT DO YOU THINK?

What this story teaches: Jesus can do anything, for He is God's Son.

1. Which of your friends could do what Jesus did for His fishermen friends? Could you?

2. Why could Jesus do this? Who was He?

The Wumpkin-Size Rock

"Widgit, Widgit. Why aren't you with Wumpkin?" Mini asked. Mini and her friends were on their way back to the big tree. As they went along Thimble-lane Trails, they found Widgit at the big Wumpkin stump.

"He left me so he could work at Wumpkin's Can Company," said Widgit. "He's canning CAN'TS so they will become CANS."

"But you're all alone," said Maxi. "Did you finish building your house in this big stump?"

"Almost," said Widgit. "But I need big Wumpkin to help me move one more rock. After all, I'm just a little Widgit. And he's such a big Wumpkin."

"Did someone mention my name?" a voice asked.

There was Wumpkin, big and smiling. His arms were loaded with tin cans.

"I didn't leave you, little Widgit," said Wumpkin. "In fact, I'm moving Wumpkin's Can Company next door to your stump house. OK?"

"OK!" said Widgit. He was so happy that he clapped his hands, or whatever Widgits have. "And I'm so glad that you're back. I need your Wumpkin power again to move a rock. And I'm asking for it."

Widgit pointed to a big Wumpkin-size rock. It was bigger than a little Widgit. But it was much smaller than a big Wumpkin.

"I CAN'T move it," said Widgit.

Wumpkin quickly grabbed Widgit's CAN'T and popped it into a can. Then he sealed the can.

"Someone CAN," said Wumpkin. "I CAN."

Wumpkin opened one of his cans, took out a CAN, and hung it on a leafy limb for Widgit to see. Widgit smiled a happy Widgit smile.

"Since you CAN, will you?" asked Widgit.

"I CAN and I WILL," said Wumpkin.

Widgit showed Wumpkin the rock. Wumpkin picked it up and tossed it into the woods.

"That was easy," said Buffy Bear.

"For a Wumpkin," said Widgit. "But not for a Widgit."

"What could you toss into the woods?" Maxi asked Widgit.

Widgit found a rock about the size of his hand. He grunted once when he picked it up. But he tossed it into the woods. "That's a Widgit-size rock," he said. "The one Wumpkin tossed is a Wumpkin-size rock."

Mini pointed to a rock almost as big as Wumpkin. "Could you toss this into the woods?" she asked.

Wumpkin laughed. "Oh, no," he said. "That's too big for a Wumpkin."

"Back home in people-land I could toss that across the yard," Maxi bragged.

Buffy Bear propped himself against the stump to think. His head was getting stuffy again.

"It takes a Widgit to move a Widgit-size rock, and a Wumpkin to move a Wumpkin-size rock," he mumbled. "Back in people-land it takes people to move a people-size rock. But what does it take to move a bigger rock?"

"A giant!" Maxi said with a laugh.

"Then who can move a still bigger rock?" asked Buffy Bear.

Everyone was quiet for a moment. Then Mini spoke.

"Jesus can," she said. "He can do anything!"

Nobody could argue with that. So Maxi, Mini, and Buffy Bear waved good-bye to Widgit and Wumpkin. Then they went on their way back to the big tree.

LET'S TALK ABOUT THIS

What this story teaches: Ask someone bigger to do bigger things. Ask Jesus to help with things too big for you.

1. Why didn't Widgit pick up the Wumpkin-size rock and toss it into the woods? What did he do?

2. What do you do when you find something too big for you to do? Do you keep on trying to do it? Do you cry? Or do you ask someone bigger to help you?

3. What will you ask Jesus to help you do today?

Fishermen Friends

Matthew 4:18–22; Mark 1:16–20; Luke 5:8–11

Peter and Andrew were still thinking about the fish they had caught as they stood on the shore. They were fishermen, and it was exciting to catch fish. But this catch was the most exciting they had ever caught. Never before had they seen anything like it. Never before had there been anything like it.

"It was a miracle!" Peter must have told Andrew a dozen times.

How could Andrew doubt that? All through the night he and Peter had fished with their friends and had caught nothing. But when Jesus came their nets began to break with fish. It *was* a miracle. Jesus had done it.

James and John stayed in the boats to mend the nets. Their father, Zebedee, came to help them. While they worked on their nets, Peter and Andrew went along the shore with small casting nets. They

were excited and wanted to catch some more fish.

"A miracle!" Peter must have mumbled as he threw his casting net again and again into the Sea of Galilee.

Then Jesus came. He stood beside Peter and Andrew. Peter wondered what Jesus would say.

"I want you to give up your fishing business," Jesus said. "Come with Me, and I will teach you to become fishers of men."

Peter and Andrew were surprised to hear what Jesus said. But Jesus must have told them that they would learn to "catch" people as they had caught fish. They would help these people follow Jesus. That would be even more exciting than catching fish.

When Jesus saw James and John mending their nets, He told them the same thing.

The fishermen friends were sorry to leave their fishing business. They were sorry to leave Zebedee. They were sorry to leave their boats. But they were happy to follow Jesus and learn what He would teach them.

WHAT DO YOU THINK?
What this story teaches: Jesus asks us to become His followers. When we do, we will help others follow Him, too.
1. What kind of work did the four friends do? Why did Jesus ask them to leave it? What would they do?
2. What did Jesus mean by "fishers of men"?

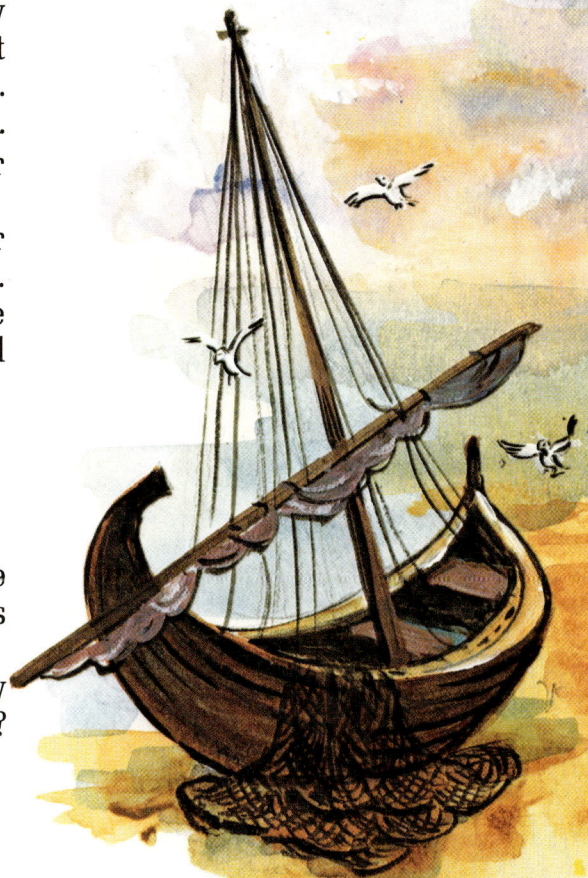

The Right Way

"I don't remember this fork in the trail," said Maxi. Mini, Maxi, and Buffy Bear were headed back to the big tree.

Maxi looked to the right. Then he looked to the left. Each part of the trail looked the same.

"But which way is the right way?" Maxi asked.

"My way," a voice said. There was Todie, sitting beside the left trail.

"If you go left you will be right," said Todie. "But if you go right, you will be left in the wrong place."

"Don't listen to him!" said Buffy Bear. "The right trail is the right trail."

"Look, I know these parts like the back of my hand," said Todie. Then he took out a big card and and stuck it in his hat.

"GUIDE," Mini read. "Are you a guide, Todie?"

"The very best," said Todie. "Follow me."

"Don't!" Buffy Bear urged. "He will lead you the wrong way. Follow me."

Maxi and Mini looked confused. They weren't sure which way to go. They weren't sure which guide to follow.

"Do you have a special guide's card?" Todie asked Buffy Bear.

Buffy Bear leaned against a tree to think about that. He felt his head getting stuffy again. "No," he said.

"Do you see me leaning against a tree to think about the right way to go?" Todie asked.

Buffy Bear felt sad. He was leaning against a tree, and Todie wasn't.

"Uh, not really," said Buffy Bear.

"See?" said Todie. "I'm your guide. Let's go."

Todie started down the left trail. He seemed so sure of himself that Maxi and Mini followed him.

"Oh, dear," said Buffy Bear. "I'm sure this is the wrong way. But I must stay with you."

Before long Maxi and Mini began to think it was the wrong way, too. Thimblelane Trails stopped being a trail. Instead, it became the edge of a pond. The pond was filled with lily pads and cattails.

"Wait! I thought you said this was the right way," Maxi called to Todie.

"It is," said Todie.

"To the big tree?" asked Mini.

"Who said anything about a big tree?" Todie asked. "This is the right way to Todie's Inn. See, there it is. Come and I'll sell you the best meal you've had."

"Bugs and flies," said Buffy Bear.

Todie hopped from one lily pad to another. "Follow me!" he called back.

But Maxi and Mini were on their way back to the fork in the road. This time they would follow the right guide. They would follow Buffy Bear back to the big tree.

LET'S TALK ABOUT THIS

What this story teaches: To find the right way, follow the right person. To find the way to God, follow Jesus.

1. Was Todie the right one to follow? Why not?
2. Whom should you follow when you want to find God? Will you? Ask Jesus to show you His way.

The Tax Collector
Matthew 9:9; Mark 2:13–14; Luke 5:27–28

People whispered when they saw Levi walking to work. They frowned as they watched him sit down at his booth by the Sea of Galilee.

Levi was a tax collector. He worked for the Romans, and the Romans ruled Levi's people. Many hated him for doing this.

Levi's work was something like that of a toll collector on an expressway today. But Levi charged more than these people do. He charged more than he should and kept much for himself, as most tax collectors did.

Whenever merchants came through Capernaum with a caravan, Levi looked at their things and charged taxes. They couldn't go on until they paid.

Levi's only friends were the other tax collectors. His neighbors hated him. None would invite him to dinner. None would go to his house to eat.

Levi did have one other friend. His name was Jesus. Whenever Jesus walked by Levi's booth, He stopped to talk. He may often have told Levi how God loved him and why He had come to earth and how Levi could follow Him.

Levi always listened carefully to Jesus. He wanted to follow Jesus. But he would have to give up his job, which brought him much money. He also wondered if his tax collector friends would stop being his friends.

There was always some weak excuse why Levi could not follow Jesus. Sometimes he would say, "Tomorrow," but it was even harder the next day to leave his rich job and his friends.

One day Levi saw Jesus coming. Crowds walked with Him, as they usually did, listening to all He said and watching all He did.

Jesus came straight up to Levi's tax booth. He smiled and greeted Levi. He looked into Levi's eyes.

"Follow Me!" Jesus said.

Levi's heart began to pound. What excuse could he give today? How could he leave this rich job? What would his friends say if he did? Would they stop being his friends?

For a moment, Levi clung to his friends and job. He just couldn't give them up! Then suddenly he realized that it was much more important to follow Jesus and be His friend.

Without a word, Levi put the money away. He closed up his tax booth. Someone else could work for the Romans now!

Then Levi looked at his tax collector friends, who by this time had gathered closer to see what he was doing. "I'm going to follow Jesus from now on," he told them. "I want you to keep on being my friends. And I want you to be Jesus' friends, too."

Levi invited all his friends to his house for dinner. He also invited Jesus. Perhaps He could talk with them and help them follow Him. Levi knew that he would follow Jesus even if his friends stopped being his friends.

The people in the crowd certainly looked surprised as they saw Levi and Jesus walk down the street together toward Levi's house. They were even more surprised as they saw Levi's tax collector friends go, too.

The tax booth looked strange and empty now. Levi had found something–Someone–much more important than that.

WHAT DO YOU THINK?

What this story teaches: To follow Jesus, Levi was willing to give up his good job and his friends. But he first tried to win them to Jesus.

1. Why was it so hard for Levi to decide to follow Jesus? What was he willing to give up? What did he think his friends would do?

2. Why did Levi invite his friends to dinner with Jesus? What did he want them to do?

3. You may remember Levi better by his other name, Matthew. Levi, a hated tax collector, became Matthew, a faithful disciple of Jesus. In time, he gave us the first book of the New Testament, a book about His friend Jesus.

Grabbie's Hats

"This way to the big tree!" said Buffy Bear. The three friends were back at the fork in the road. This time Maxi and Mini were going to follow the right person. And they would go on the right trail.

"Let's go!" said Buffy Bear.

Before long the three friends came to the two booths where GiGi and Grabbie had been. Maxi and Mini wanted to see what Grabbie was doing. Had he changed his sign?

"There it is!" said Mini. "Grabbie's Giving Service right next to GiGi's Giving Service."

"He did change his sign," said Maxi. "From now on he will be a giver instead of a taker."

"How do you know?" asked Buffy Bear.

"Because the sign says so," said Maxi.

"Does that make it so?" asked Buffy Bear.

Mini looked surprised. She had not thought of Grabbie's going back to his grabbing ways. Maxi looked surprised, too. He had thought for sure that Grabbie would keep on with his giving service.

"If Grabbie is really going to run a giving service, he MUST give up his old grabby ways," said Maxi.

"Just as a person who follows Jesus must give up his old sinful ways," said Mini.

"But how can we help Grabbie give up his old ways?" Maxi asked.

"Let's ask GiGi," said Mini. "She will know if Grabbie is still grabby."

GiGi was happy to see her friends again. She invited them into her GiGi's Giving Service booth.

"Grabbie has not tried to grab any more of my golden eggs," said GiGi.

"But what has he done with the golden eggs he took from you before?" asked Maxi.

"I guess he still has them," said GiGi. "And I guess he still has something else he shouldn't have."

Maxi and Mini looked surprised. "What?" they asked.

"The hats!" said GiGi. "He tricked me with those hats. They helped him in his grabby ways."

"Oh, no!" said Maxi. "He must get rid of those hats. If he doesn't, he may be tempted to go back to his grabby ways with them."

Grabbie smiled when he saw the four friends again. But he was ashamed when Mini and GiGi picked up some of the golden eggs. They said nothing. They did not need to say anything. Grabbie knew what they were thinking.

Grabbie was ashamed when Maxi and Buffy Bear picked up his hats, one by one. They said nothing. They did not need to say anything. Grabbie knew what they were thinking.

"I changed the sign outside!" he said. Grabbie pointed to the sign. He had marked out "Grabbing" and painted in "Giving." Now it read Grabbie's Giving Service, not Grabbie's Grabbing Service.

But the four friends – Maxi, Mini, GiGi, and Buffy Bear – said nothing. Grabbie knew what they were thinking.

"I…uh…have been thinking about some people who need those golden eggs," he said, "I just haven't had the time to give them away yet."

Grabbie watched Mini and GiGi as he said that. It was a silly excuse. He knew it, and he knew that Mini and GiGi knew it. He was even more ashamed now.

"I…uh…should have given those hats away," he said. "I guess I won't be needing them anymore. But they seem too nice to just give away."

Grabbie watched Maxi and Buffy Bear as he said that. It was a silly excuse. He knew it, and he knew that Maxi and Buffy Bear knew it. He was even more ashamed now.

"But I PROMISED to give up my grabby ways," he argued. It was still another silly excuse.

Grabbie looked at his four friends. They looked at him. Then Grabbie looked at the floor.

"I…uh…well…uh…" Grabbie tried to think of one last silly excuse. But every one he thought of was too silly to say.

"It's time to give some things away," he said. "Want to help me give away some hats and golden eggs?"

The four friends smiled. Of course they would help Grabbie give those things away. They would do almost anything to keep him from going back to his old grabby ways.

LET'S TALK ABOUT THIS
What this story teaches: To follow a new way, you must give up the old. To follow Jesus, you must give up your old sinful ways.

1. Why did Grabbie keep his hats and golden eggs? Why did his friends want him to give them away?

2. When a person accepts Jesus as Savior, why is it so important to give up the old ways?

TO ALL THE WORLD

Good News for Everyone

Acts 13: 6-12

The believers in Antioch were excited. The good news about Jesus really *was* good news. Those who believed in Jesus were suddenly different.

Some began to share their money and food. Others began to pray together. Still others went everywhere to tell people about Jesus.

The good news was too good to keep in Antioch only!

One day when some believers were praying together, the Holy Spirit spoke to them. "I have a special work for Paul and Barnabas," He told them.

The believers prayed some more. They would not even eat food. Then they had a church service at Antioch.

During this service the believers put their hands on Paul and Barnabas. They prayed for them and sent them to take the good news to faraway places.

Paul and Barnabas went to the seaport not far from Antioch. They boarded a ship and sailed for the island of Cyprus. Barnabas had lived there at one time, so he knew where they should go.

When Paul and Barnabas landed at Cyprus, they went across the island, preaching in the towns as they went. At last they arrived at Paphos, where the governor of the island lived.

The governor had heard about Paul and Barnabas. He had heard about the good news of Jesus. He wanted to hear more, so he invited Paul and Barnabas to visit him.

Of course, Paul and Barnabas were happy to visit the governor. They were happy to share their good news with him. The governor, Sergius Paulus, was a wise man. If he would accept Jesus, he would probably share the good news with others.

But the governor was not alone. A sorcerer was with him that day. This man, who was a fake prophet, had two names, Bar-jesus and Elymas.

Elymas did not like what Paul and Barnabas told the governor. People who accepted Jesus did not accept fake prophets like Elymas. If the governor be-

came a believer, he would certainly never listen to this man again.

"Don't listen to these men," Elymas kept telling the governor. "Don't believe what they are saying."

Whenever Paul and Barnabas tried to talk about Jesus, Elymas tried to stop them. Whenever they urged the governor to believe in Jesus, he urged the governor not to believe.

After this went on awhile, Paul turned angrily to Elymas. "You surely are the devil's son," Paul told Elymas. "All you want to do is work against the Lord. We've had enough of your evil tricks. At this moment, the Lord will punish you. He will make you blind!"

As soon as Paul said that, Elymas was struck blind. He began wandering around. He begged for someone to take his hand and lead him.

The governor was amazed to see what happened. Now he knew that God was with Paul and Barnabas. The good news they offered was from God, not from themselves.

So the governor believed. The good news was for the people of Cyprus as well as the people of Antioch!

WHAT DO YOU THINK?
What this story teaches: The good news about Jesus is for everyone. It is too good to keep to ourselves.

1. How did the people of Antioch feel about the good news? Why did they want to share it with others?
2. What did Elymas do to keep the governor from believing in Jesus? What happened to Elymas then?
3. Was the good news for the people of Antioch only? Whom is it for?

GiGi's Good News Service

"Well, well!" said GiGi. "Grabbie's Giving Service is certainly doing well. He gave all his hats and golden eggs to the neediest folks we could find."

"Yes, and that was fun to help him," said Mini. "But what about you? What will you do with GiGi's Giving Service?"

"We don't need two giving services next to each other," said GiGi. "I should start a new business."

"Like what?" asked Buffy Bear.

"Like I don't know what," said GiGi. "Do you?"

"I do," said Maxi. "Thimblelane Trails needs a news service."

"A news service?" said GiGi. "But I don't even know what that is."

"When I have something to tell, I need someone to tell it," said Maxi. "That's a news service."

"Do you have something to tell?" asked GiGi.

"I have something good to tell," said Maxi.

"Does that mean you need a good news service?" asked GiGi.

"What I have to tell is more than good," said Maxi. "It's the best! It's even better than best. It's called THE GOOD NEWS."

"Then you need a good news service," said GiGi. "That really sounds important. Who is this good news for?"

"Everyone!" said Maxi.

"Everyone?" asked GiGi. "And what is this good news for everyone?"

"It's the good news about Jesus," said Maxi. "Jesus came to die for us. Everyone who believes in Him and accepts Him as Savior will become a Christian. Christians live for Jesus now. Someday we will live with Him in His home in heaven."

"First, we must change the sign," said Mini. "Then everyone will know that GiGi is in the good news business."

"We'll call it GiGi's Good News Service," said Maxi.

"But what do I do then?" asked GiGi. "A calico goose isn't exactly the best one to share your good news."

"We'll print a good-news-for-everyone paper," said Maxi. "Mini and I will write the paper and get it printed. Then you can share it with everyone who comes along Thimblelane Trails."

GiGi was excited. It would be much better to have a good news service than a giving service. Of course she would be the first to read this good news.

Everyone went to work. GiGi and Buffy Bear scratched out the word "Giving" in GiGi's sign. Then they put in the words "Good News."

Maxi and Mini began to write the good-news paper. Before long they had finished it. Then they had it printed, and it was ready for GiGi to give to everyone who came by GiGi's Good News Service.

"GiGi's Good News Service is now in business," said GiGi. It was a happy day for everyone!

LET'S TALK ABOUT THIS

What this story teaches: The good news about Jesus is for everyone. It is too good to keep to ourselves.

1. What is the good news that Maxi mentioned? Why is it such good news?

2. What did Maxi and Mini want to do with their good news? Keep it? Or share it? Why?

3. Have you heard the good news about Jesus? Have you accepted Him as your Savior? If so, what do you want to do with your good news? If not, what would you like to do about that now?

Good News for Lystra

Acts 14: 8-20

Paul and Barnabas were far from their home church at Antioch. They were in a town called Lystra, telling the people there about Jesus.

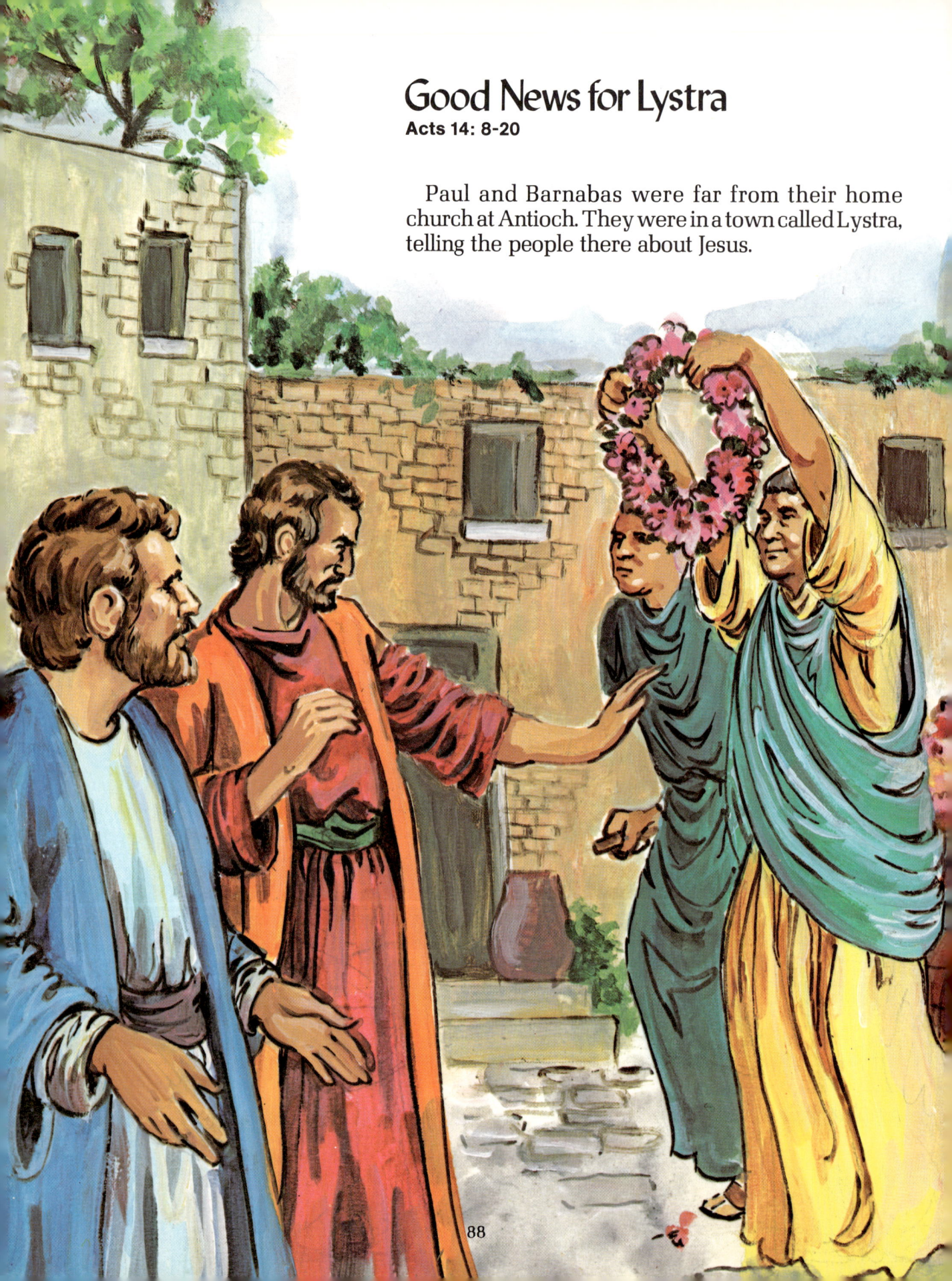

These two men had told people in many towns about Jesus. Some believed in Him. Others were so angry at what they said that they drove the two out of their town.

One day Paul was preaching to a group of people at Lystra. He saw one man staring at him. He listened to everything Paul said. Then Paul saw that the man had crippled feet. His feet had been that way since he was born.

Paul watched the man as he preached. *That man is ready to believe in Jesus!* Paul thought.

Paul stopped preaching. He looked into the man's eyes. "Stand up!" he said.

The man stood up. He walked. He had never done that before.

"I can walk! I can walk!" he shouted to his friends and neighbors.

The friends and neighbors were certainly surprised. This man had always been crippled. Now in a moment he could walk.

Suddenly everyone began to look at Paul and Barnabas. These men had healed a cripple!

"They are gods!" someone shouted. Soon everyone was shouting.

"They are gods! They are gods!" they cried out.

"That one is Jupiter!" some said, pointing at Paul.

"That one is Mercury!" said others, pointing at Barnabas.

There was a temple in Lystra where the people worshiped Jupiter. A priest was in charge there. When he heard that Jupiter had come to town, he ran out to see.

The priest brought cartloads of flowers to Paul and Barnabas. "Jupiter is here with us! Mercury has come with him," the priest shouted.

Soon things went from bad to worse. The crowd was getting too excited. They wanted to sacrifice oxen to Paul and Barnabas.

"Stop! Stop!" Paul and Barnabas shouted. "What are you doing? We are not gods. We are men, just like you. But we have some good news for you."

Paul and Barnabas tried to tell the people about Jesus. They told the people that they had come to share the good news about Jesus with them.

One by one, the people stopped shouting. One by one, they turned away and went home. Who wanted to shout and get excited about two men? Who wanted to bring cartloads of flowers to men like themselves? Who wanted to sacrifice oxen to these men if they really were not Jupiter and Mercury?

At last Paul and Barnabas stood alone in the streets of Lystra. Everyone else had gone home.

A few days later the same people were in the streets again. They were listening to Paul and Barnabas tell

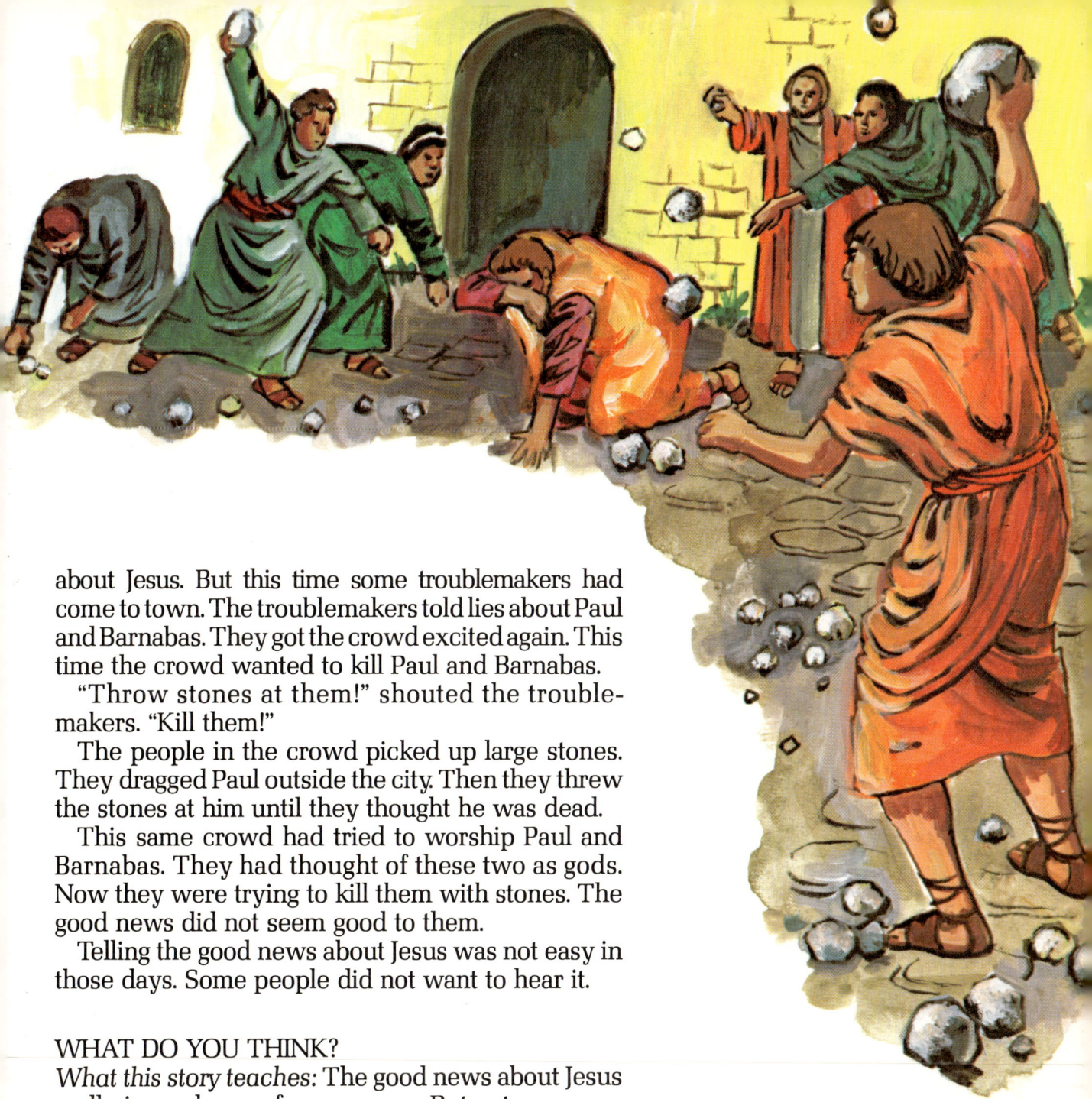

about Jesus. But this time some troublemakers had come to town. The troublemakers told lies about Paul and Barnabas. They got the crowd excited again. This time the crowd wanted to kill Paul and Barnabas.

"Throw stones at them!" shouted the troublemakers. "Kill them!"

The people in the crowd picked up large stones. They dragged Paul outside the city. Then they threw the stones at him until they thought he was dead.

This same crowd had tried to worship Paul and Barnabas. They had thought of these two as gods. Now they were trying to kill them with stones. The good news did not seem good to them.

Telling the good news about Jesus was not easy in those days. Some people did not want to hear it.

WHAT DO YOU THINK?

What this story teaches: The good news about Jesus really is good news for everyone. But not everyone wants to hear it.

1. What did the crowd at Lystra think about Paul and Barnabas at first? What did they think about them when they learned that Paul and Barnabas were men with good news about Jesus?

2. What happened when troublemakers came to Lystra? What did the crowd do then? What does this tell you about the way some people receive Jesus' good news?

The Good News Gazette

"I'm so excited," GiGi the calico goose said. "Look at that beautiful sign."

It was a nice sign. GiGi and Buffy Bear had worked hard to change it so that it read GiGi's Good News Service.

"But where are the copies of the good-news paper?" asked Buffy Bear.

"Here!" said Maxi. "While you and GiGi were working on the sign, Mini and I were working on the good-news paper. We have called it *The Good News Gazette*."

"It tells the good news about Jesus," said Mini.

"And that's good news for everyone," Maxi added.

"So everyone along Thimblelane Trails should want to hear it," said Mini.

"OK, let's open shop!" said GiGi. "As soon as we do, everyone will come running to hear this good news."

GiGi opened the shop windows. Buffy Bear stacked the copies of *The Good News Gazette* neatly on the counter. Then Maxi and Mini began to shout.

"Good news! Good news!" they cried out. "Come and get the good news!"

Two of the folks along Thimblelane Trails poked their heads around some trees. They saw *The Good News Gazette*. But they would not come to GiGi's Good News Service to see it and hear about the good news.

Two others came near the booth. But as soon as Maxi said something to them, they went the other way. They would not even let him tell about the good news.

Two more came to the booth. They picked up *The Good News Gazette* and read the good news. But they shook their heads and went away without the gazette. "Who wants that kind of news?" they asked. "We can't believe that!"

Two others came to the booth. They also read the gazette. They even took a copy with them. But before they had gone very far down Thimblelane Trails, they threw their copy of the gazette on a pile of leaves.

At last two came who read the gazette and took it with them, smiling as they talked. "This sounds like good news for us!" they said.

GiGi looked sad. "I thought this was good news," she said.

"It is," said Maxi.

"But I thought this was good news for everyone!" GiGi added.

"It is," said Mini.

"Then why doesn't everyone accept it gladly?" asked GiGi.

Maxi and Mini thought a long time about that. "It IS good news," said Maxi. "And it IS good news for everyone."

"Then everyone should want it," GiGi said again. "Everyone should accept it gladly. So why don't they?"

"You're right!" said Maxi. "They should. But not everyone wants it. Some folks just won't listen. Others think the good news is not good for them. Others think it is, but then let other things become more important."

"Then I suppose we should close up shop," said GiGi.

"Would you keep it open for ten folks who accept the good news?" Maxi asked.

"Oh, yes," said GiGi.

"For five?" asked Maxi.

"Yes, of course," GiGi answered.

"How about for one?" said Maxi.

GiGi frowned. Would she? Yes, of course she would. "I would keep it open for just one," she said. "So I will keep it open, for I'm sure that more than one will accept the good news. Thank you for helping me see this."

Buffy Bear tugged at Maxi's sleeve. "Look!" he said, "the sun is setting. We must get back to the big tree."

Maxi, Mini, and Buffy Bear waved good-bye and hurried back to the big tree where they had started. They went into the big hole at the bottom. Buffy Bear sat down.

"You two think of home, and you'll soon be back there," he said. "I'll be waiting for you there."

In a moment Maxi and Mini were going back up through the dark tree. They felt themselves growing to full size again. As they came from the hole at the top of the big tree, they saw Poppi, waiting at the picnic table.

"Did you find Buffy Bear?" Poppi asked.

"Oh, yes," said Mini. "And I know just where to find him now."

Mini ran to the other side of the tree. There was the big hole at the bottom, exactly like the one that she had seen along Thimblelane Trails. And there was Buffy Bear, sitting in the hole, waiting for her. But now he was the stuffed animal Buffy Bear that she kept on her bedroom shelf.

Mini hugged her stuffed Buffy Bear. Then she put him back on the shelf in her room with her stuffed Todie, GiGi, Grabbie, Widgit, Wumpkin, and Snoggy. Mini lay on her bed and looked at these friends. They seemed so real now, for she thought of all the fun she had had with them along Thimblelane Trails. Perhaps some day she and Maxi could go back!

LET'S TALK ABOUT THIS

What this story teaches: The good news about Jesus really IS good news for everyone. But not everyone wants to hear it.

1. Why was GiGi disappointed when she set up her Good News Service? What happened?

2. Is the good news about Jesus really good news for everyone? Why then don't some people want it?

3. Is the good news about Jesus good news for you? Have you received it? Have you received Jesus as YOUR Savior?

Mini's Word List

Twelve words that all Minis and Maxis want to know:

BOTTLES – Most bottles today are made of glass or plastic. They come in many shapes and sizes. But in Bible times only a few rich people had glass bottles. They were hard to make. And they cost too much. Most bottles were pottery jugs or jars made of clay, or were made of animal skins. These skins, often from a goat, were sewed around the edges except for one opening. Water or wine was poured in or out of this opening.

CANAAN – Through the time of the Old Testament, the land of Palestine was ruled by many different kinds of people. The borders of the land changed often. "Palestine" and "Canaan" were two different names for the same land. Today Israel rules most of this same land.

DEVIL – The devil is Satan, God's powerful enemy. He is also our enemy and tries to get us to do wrong things, things that hurt God. The devil wants people to sin. When we sin we help the devil and hurt God.

GOOD NEWS – The news about Jesus is good news. It is sometimes called the gospel, which means the same. It is good news that Jesus came. It is good news that He lived the kind of life we should live. It is good news that he taught His disciples, and us, how to please God. But the best news of all is that He died for us and rose from the dead. This makes it possible for us to come to God through Him. It makes it possible for us to live with Him forever.

KING – Many kings, such as King Saul, King David, and King Solomon were rulers over the whole nation. But many other kings in Bible times were like mayors, for they ruled over a city. Or they were like governors, for they ruled over a small region.

OLIVES – Bible-time olives were like the ones you buy in the grocery store today. The oil squeezed from them was like the olive oil in today's stores. But it was used in much different ways. Olive oil was most widely used in lamps to give light in homes or other buildings. Sometimes perfume was mixed with it, and it was used on the skin.

PREACH – When a speaker talks to a crowd of people, he speaks. But when he talks about God or His Word, he preaches.

PRINCE – A king's son. The oldest son was usually the one to become the next king.

SEA OF GALILEE – A lake about sixty miles north of Jerusalem. It is about eight miles wide and about 150 feet deep. Many events in Jesus' life happened around this lake. The region around it is called Galilee.

SORCERER – A person who claimed to have powers that an ordinary person did not have. Sometimes this person worked with evil spirits and evil magic. There were many sorcerers in Bible times.

TAX COLLECTOR – A person who collected taxes for the government. In Jesus' time this person worked for the Romans, not the Jewish people of the land. So they were hated, just as the Romans were hated.

WORSHIP – Often we talk about worshiping God. That means we honor Him. In some way we show Him that we believe He is God and that we are His people.